MAKING S-P-A-C-E FOR
WHAT MATTERS MOST

MAKING
S-P-A-C-E
FOR WHAT MATTERS
MOST

The Work-Life Balance Guide

SHALU AGGARWAL

WESTLAND
BUSINESS

WESTLAND
BUSINESS

Published by Westland Business, an imprint of Westland Books, a division of Nasadiya Technologies Private Limited, in 2025

No. 269/2B, First Floor, 'Irai Arul', Vimalraj Street, Nethaji Nagar, Alapakkam Main Road, Maduravoyal, Chennai 600095

Westland, the Westland logo, Westland Business and the Westland Business logo are the trademarks of Nasadiya Technologies Private Limited, or its affiliates.

Copyright © Shalu Aggarwal, 2025

Shalu Aggarwal asserts the moral right to be identified as the author of this work.

ISBN: 9789371970150

10 9 8 7 6 5 4 3 2

The views and opinions expressed in this work are the author's own and the facts are as reported by her, and the publisher is in no way liable for the same.

All rights reserved

Typeset by Jojy Philip
Printed at Thomson Press (India) Ltd

No part of this book may be reproduced, or stored in a retrieval system, or transmitted in any form or by any means, electronic, mechanical, photocopying, recording, or otherwise, without express written permission of the publisher.

CONTENTS

Living the Balance: My Own Journey Today — vii

1. Understanding Work-Life Balance — 1
2. The Wake-Up Call: The Moment of Realisation — 7
3. Tools for Efficiency: From Chaos to Control — 13
4. The Art of Delegation: Empowering Your Team — 21
5. Self-Care: Your Foundation for Success — 30
6. Family and Relationships: The Heart of Balance — 33
7. Giving Back: Creating a Purpose Beyond Profit — 40
8. Continuous Learning: Growing Beyond the Ordinary — 47
9. Creating a Positive Workplace Culture — 54
10. The Power of Saying 'No' — 62
11. Systems, Technology and the Power of Doing It Right — 68
12. Wealth Management: Securing Your Future — 71
13. Living the Balance — 79

LIVING THE BALANCE: MY OWN JOURNEY TODAY

As I write this, I am in Switzerland with my husband, who is undergoing a two-month medical treatment. Back home, it's the end of the financial year—a time that usually brings stress, deadlines and late nights for most business owners.

But today, even in the middle of a family health crisis, in a different country, in a different time zone. I am at peace.

Zoom calls, timely reporting and a responsible team have ensured that my absence isn't a disruption. Instead, it has become a chance for the team to rise, to lead and to shine. And they have done it with incredible grace.

This peace wasn't accidental. It was built over years of learning, applying systems, trusting people and letting go of control. Balance like this is earned, not given.

For a long time, I believed I had mastered work-life balance because I was managing everything—home, business and family. But I eventually realised that being busy isn't the same as being balanced. True balance lets you grow without burning out, give without losing yourself and lead without feeling overwhelmed.

I experienced this first-hand in 2016, when I entered one of the many ventures of the Action Group—the EVA slipper unit, my husband Ajay Aggarwal's first entrepreneurial dream. What began as a few hours of support became a full-time calling. Today, this unit feels like my third child. It's not just a workplace—it's a family built on shared values, trust and care.

I've been fortunate to walk this journey with the support of my husband, my in-laws and my two sons, Krish and Kanish. Their faith in me gave me the strength to lead with both heart and structure. And I'd like to thank my parents for raising me with a positive mindset and a heart that seeks happiness, even through challenges.

That's why I decided to write this book—to bring together the stories, tools, reflections and practices that helped me—and may help you too.

This isn't just my story—it's the story of so many of us trying to balance ambition with relationships, responsibility with rest. It's a reminder that balance is not about slowing down success. It's about building a life that can hold both ambition and compassion at the same time.

This book is not about perfection. It's about progress. It's about making space for what matters—without guilt, without burnout and without losing sight of who we are.

To my team, my mentors, my friends and my family back home—thank you. Your presence, love and support are the invisible systems that make everything else possible.

If even one idea in this book helps you breathe easier, think clearer or feel less alone in your journey—then this was worth writing.

With love and gratitude,
Shalu Aggarwal
Switzerland, March 2025

CHAPTER 1

UNDERSTANDING WORK-LIFE BALANCE

What is Work-Life Balance?

Work-life balance is not about working less or relaxing more. It's about intentional alignment. It's the ability to manage your professional goals without sacrificing your personal values and relationships. It's about living a life where your work supports your well-being, not undermines it.

> **True balance means:**
> 1. You honour your commitments—at work and at home.
> 2. You take care of your health, mind and spirit.
> 3. You stay productive without feeling drained or guilty.
> 4. You feel present, not pulled in all directions.

It's important to understand that balance is not constant: it's fluid. Some days your business may demand more time; other days, your family might. What matters is being aware and intentional about how you spend your time and energy, and making choices that reflect your true priorities. Most importantly, your definition of balance is unique. What feels balanced to you might not look balanced to someone else—and that's okay.

Tool: The Balance Scorecard (Personal Edition)

This tool helps you assess your overall well-being across four essential areas of life. It's adapted from the corporate strategy world but simplified for personal clarity.

✓ **Category**

Guiding Questions

WORK & CAREER
Am I growing and contributing meaningfully in my profession?

FAMILY & RELATIONSHIPS
Are my relationships strong, loving and supported?

HEALTH & WELLNESS
Am I taking care of my body, mind and energy?

PERSONAL FULFILLMENT
Am I pursuing passions, learning or giving back?

How to Use It

1. Reflect on each area honestly.
2. Give yourself a score out of 10 based on current satisfaction (10 being the best).
3. Identify which area needs more attention.
4. Take one small action this week to improve the lowest-scoring area.

For instance:

If your 'Health & Wellness' score is low, commit to a 20-minute daily walk or a weekly yoga class. Small steps can create big changes.

Reflection Questions

- Which area of your balance scorecard needs improvement most right now?
- What's one habit or change you can implement this week to begin realigning your balance?

Real-Life Inspiration
Dhirubhai Ambani: Vision Rooted in Family

Dhirubhai Ambani built one of India's largest and most influential business empires from the ground up. But what truly set him apart wasn't just his entrepreneurial genius: it was his deep-rooted sense of family, tradition and legacy.

Dhirubhai Ambani
Founder of Reliance

Despite leading Reliance to dizzying heights, he stayed grounded in family values. He maintained strong personal relationships and involved his sons, Mukesh and Anil, in the business early— Dhirubhai Ambani was not exactly known for clear succession planning which is what is supposed to have led to a feud between his two sons to nurture shared vision and responsibility.

He was known to spend personal time mentoring his sons, instilling in them not just business tactics but the importance of ethics, simplicity and loyalty. Even amid massive business pressures, he made time for emotional bonding and family rituals, showing us that business ambition and personal connection can—and should—coexist.

He represents the very idea of sustainable success—one that grows from a balanced foundation of values, family and purpose.

Closing Thoughts

Balance isn't something you find once and keep forever. It's something you create, adjust and protect—every day.

'Balance is not better time management, but better boundary management.'
—Betsy Jacobson

CHAPTER 2

THE WAKE-UP CALL—THE MOMENT OF REALISATION

For the longest time, I believed I had mastered work–life balance. I was constantly on the move—working from morning to evening, handling multiple activities at work, managing our diverse businesses and trying to be present in a joint family that spanned four generations. My days were packed, and I thought this constant busyness meant I was being productive. I truly believed I was doing everything right.

> **But the truth was quite different.**
>
> At work, I was giving my time—but I wasn't truly productive. I was involved in every small task without questioning whether it needed my attention. I thought I was being hard-working but in reality, I was overworking and under-delegating.

I had taken charge of everything—right from strategic decisions to minor operational matters. I believed that being involved in every detail showed commitment, but it actually revealed a lack of systems and trust in the team.

The Moment that Shifted My Perspective

One evening, after a long day at work, I was still on the phone at home, coordinating unimportant tasks, answering vendor queries and reviewing day-to-day operations. I didn't even realise that my husband, who was dealing with his own health challenges, had been watching me.

He gently pointed it out—not with judgement, but out of care.

He said, 'You're doing the same things you did during the day—still solving the same little problems. Even when you're home, you're not really here.'

> **And then he made a suggestion that would change the course of my life.**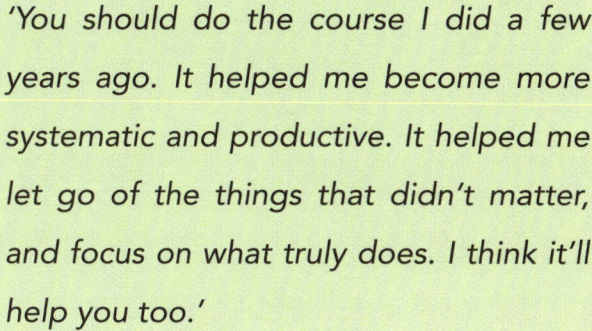
>
> 'You should do the course I did a few years ago. It helped me become more systematic and productive. It helped me let go of the things that didn't matter, and focus on what truly does. I think it'll help you too.'

At first, I brushed it off. I thought I was already efficient. But his words stayed with me. I knew he wasn't criticising me—he was opening a door to a better version of myself.

What I Learnt
That course was just the beginning of a complete mindset shift.

I learnt many things through it—tools, techniques and, most importantly, a new way of thinking. While I will be sharing these in detail throughout the book, what stood out most was this:

If we keep working the same way we've always worked, we'll keep getting the same results.

We often continue old patterns without questioning them, whether out of habit, pride or fear. But when we desire different results—more peace, better health, improved efficiency or deeper relationships—we must change how we think and how we work.

And to Change What We Do, We Must First Become More Aware and More Learned

That course opened my eyes. It taught me that learning and staying updated is not optional—it's essential. The world is evolving, and so must we. If we want our businesses and lives to grow, we need to invest in ourselves first.

That one course led to another. I started reading books, attending seminars, listening to experts and absorbing every piece of wisdom I could. And as I grew, I started making changes—small ones at first, and then larger ones.

What I've learnt through that journey—practical tools, time-tested systems and personal insights—is what I'll be sharing in this book. Because balance isn't just about managing time. It's about growing with time.

Reflection Questions

- Are you taking on tasks that others can or should be doing?
- Have you ever confused being busy with being productive?
- What is one small change you can make this week to reclaim your time and presence?

Real-Life Inspiration
Steve Jobs: The Crisis that Brought Clarity

Steve Jobs, one of the most iconic innovators of our time, was known for his pursuit of perfection and relentless drive. But after his cancer diagnosis, his entire outlook changed.

In his famous Stanford commencement speech, he said: *'Your time is limited, so don't waste it living someone else's life.'*

STEVE JOBS
Founder of Apple

His health crisis brought clarity. He started prioritising family, simplicity, and meaning over prestige. Jobs realised that success without presence is empty, and legacy without love is incomplete.

CHAPTER 3

TOOLS FOR EFFICIENCY: FROM CHAOS TO CONTROL

When I was actively managing multiple verticals of our business—production, marketing, sales, HR, accounts—I used to feel proud of being involved in everything. I thought multitasking and doing it all myself made me a strong leader.

But in reality, it left me overwhelmed and exhausted. Every day felt like firefighting. I was working hard but not necessarily working smart. My to-do list never ended, and important work was often postponed in favour of urgent-but-unimportant tasks.

What I needed wasn't more hours in the day. I needed better clarity and structure. This chapter is about the exact tools and systems I began using after my wake-up call. These tools helped me move from chaos to clarity, from being busy to being effective.

Why Efficiency Matters in Work-life Balance

Efficiency isn't about squeezing more into your day, it's about doing what matters most and letting go of what doesn't. When you become more efficient:

- You free up mental space
- You make better decisions
- You create more time for yourself and your family
- You feel a sense of control instead of constant catch-up

Productivity with intention leads to peace.

Tool 1: The Eisenhower Matrix— Prioritise with Purpose

One of the simplest and most powerful tools I learnt during my course was the Eisenhower matrix. It helped me realise how many tasks I was spending time on that didn't need my involvement at all.

Here's how it works:

THE MATRIX	URGENT	NOT URGENT
IMPORTANT	Do Now	Schedule
NOT IMPORTANT	Delegate	Eliminate or avoid

Examples

- Urgent + Important: Crisis at work, deadlines, client emergencies
- Not Urgent + Important: Planning, team building, learning
- Urgent + Not Important: Interruptions, minor issues, approvals
- Not Urgent + Not Important: Gossip, social scrolling, busywork

A Personal Lesson in Letting Go

I used to think doing everything myself made me a better leader.

One year, during our annual retailer scheme, I was expected to choose reward items like lunch boxes or electronics—something I always insisted on doing personally. But I had to travel to Kerala for my husband's treatment, so I delegated the task to my team for the first time. They not only handled it well, they exceeded expectations with better choices and better pricing.

That experience helped me realise that not everything marked 'urgent and Important' truly needs my time. I began applying the Eisenhower matrix to consciously delegate, defer and focus only on what truly required my attention. This clarity freed up my time for strategic work—like launching our new school shoe line with anti-germ technology, which led to significant business growth.

My Takeaway

Delegating isn't losing control, it's creating space to lead where it matters most.

Your Goal

Spend more time in the Not Urgent but Important quadrant. That's where growth, planning, health and peace live

**Tool 2: Time Blocking—
Take Control of Your Calendar**

Most of us let the day control us. Time blocking flips that. It allows you to proactively design your day.

1. Identify your top 3–5 priorities for the day or week.
2. Estimate how much time each one needs.
3. Block that time on your calendar—including time for breaks, family, learning and yourself.
4. Treat those blocks like appointments. Honour them.

Tip

Start your day with the most important work—not emails or messages. Reserve mornings for focused tasks and afternoons for meetings or coordination.

Tool 3: The 'Stop Doing' List

We all have to-do lists. But very few of us maintain a stop-doing list—a list of activities we need to eliminate or delegate.

Ask Yourself

- What am I doing that someone else can do 80 per cent as well?

- What tasks drain my energy but don't add value?
- What recurring things take up time without meaningful return?

An Example from My Life

I used to personally approve every petty cash expense. It made me feel in control, but it drained my time. Today, that's handled by our finance system and team with clear thresholds and audits. Letting go isn't losing control—it's gaining focus.

- What are your biggest distractions during the day?
- What tasks are you doing that someone else could do just as well?
- Are your daily actions aligned with your long-term goals?

Real-Life Inspiration
Warren Buffett: The Power of Focus

Warren Buffett is one of the most productive and successful investors in the world. What's his secret? Extreme focus.

He once said,
'The difference between successful people and very successful people is that very successful people say no to almost everything.'

WARREN BUFFETT
Chairperson of Berkshire Hathaway

Buffett doesn't waste time on distractions. He delegates operational work, focuses on his strengths and protects his time fiercely. His schedule is shockingly empty, and that's the point.

Why this example matters here
Because it shows that efficiency isn't about doing more; it's about doing less, better.

Closing Thoughts

If you feel overwhelmed, it's not because you're weak, it's because your systems need strengthening.

Start small. Pick one tool from this chapter and try it for one week. Notice what shifts. Then build from there.

Being busy is not the same as being productive. Productivity is getting the right things done, not doing everything.

CHAPTER 4

THE ART OF DELEGATION: EMPOWERING YOUR TEAM

There was a time when I believed that being a good leader meant being involved in every little detail. I thought I had to supervise everything personally, from approving designs and checking packaging to following up on dispatches and coordinating staff schedules. I wore 'hardworking' like a badge of honour. But over time, I realised something very important:

I wasn't leading. I was limiting.

I was limiting my team's growth, my company's scalability and, most of all, my own peace of mind. The breakthrough came when I finally understood the power of delegation.

Why Delegation is not a Weakness

Many business leaders, especially those who have grown businesses from the ground up, hesitate to delegate. We feel like no one else can do it the way we can.

> **But in reality:**
> - Trying to do it all makes you the bottleneck.
> - It creates dependency in the team instead of capability.
> - And it leads to burnout—emotional, mental and even physical.

Delegation isn't about offloading work—it's about elevating yourself and others. It allows you to focus on high-impact tasks while empowering others to grow.

My Turning Point

I realised that the problem wasn't that I didn't have people to support me; the problem was me. I didn't trust others with responsibility. I hadn't built the systems to delegate effectively. I hadn't even trained people for roles beyond execution.

The first change I made was hiring an Executive Assistant. Initially, I felt guilty about it. How could I let someone else manage my calendar, meetings and communication? But gradually, I saw the magic. I had more time, more energy and more mental space for strategy, creativity and growth.

Then I worked with my team leads to redefine roles and responsibilities. We set up weekly reporting systems, daily check-ins and clear escalation paths. The more I stepped back strategically, the more the team stepped up operationally.

Tool: The Delegation Matrix

This tool helped me decide what to keep and what to delegate:

TASK TYPE	ACTION
• Important, and I'm the best person to do it	**Do it myself**
• Important but someone else can do it	**Delegate**
• Not important but urgent	**Delegate or delay**
• Not important and not urgent	**Eliminate**

Steps to Use It

1. Make a list of your weekly tasks.
2. Categorise them using the matrix above.
3. Identify at least three tasks you can delegate immediately.
4. Assign, train and trust, then review results weekly.

What I Gained by Delegating

- Time to think strategically
- Space to learn and grow
- Freedom to spend more time with my family
- A more confident and capable team
- Faster decision-making and better execution

A Story That Changed Everything

As I shared in the previous chapter, one of the most eye-opening moments came when I stepped back from choosing reward items for our annual retailer scheme, a task I used to micromanage.

That small shift showed me something big: when you delegate with trust, your team often surprises you with excellence. It wasn't just about handing over a task. It was about changing my role from a doer to an enabler.

Delegation isn't a sign of weakness—it's a reflection of clarity, systems and shared ownership.

And this was just the beginning. After that, I consciously started stepping back from many things that didn't need my time, things anyone else could handle just as well. Instead of getting involved in decisions from the beginning, I positioned myself as the final approver when required.

With every step back, I discovered something beautiful.

Most of what I was doing wasn't what was needed from my seat. And when I let go of that, something shifted. I had more space for myself, for high-value strategic thinking and for the actual role I was meant to play as a managing director, i.e., to expand the business and make it more profitable.

> **In the beginning, I was all over the place!**
>
> Back in 2016, when I first began working, my schedule was quite disorganised. I used to take random, scattered meetings throughout the day. There was no structure and, most of the time, I would forget to follow up on what was discussed.

Eventually, I started following up myself, but even that became overwhelming.

So I shifted again. I empowered my Executive Assistant to follow up with each department and remind me of key points. I also moved from daily informal meetings to scheduled weekly reviews with each department.

And the transformation was incredible.

These meetings became more focused. The team knew what to prepare. They began setting their own targets. They took more ownership. Their accountability and leadership improved because they were no longer waiting for instructions—they were leading from the front.

True delegation isn't just task transfer—it's mindset transformation.

 **Reflection Questions**

❓ What are you holding on to that someone else can handle?

❓ Are you empowering your team or unknowingly creating dependency?

❓ What is one task you can delegate starting this week?

Real-Life Inspiration
Indra Nooyi: Leading with Trust

As the former CEO of PepsiCo, **Indra Nooyi** led one of the world's most successful companies. She's admired not just for her strategic brilliance but also for her ability to empower her team.

Nooyi led one of the world's most successful companies. She's admired not just for her strategic brilliance but also for her ability to empower her team.

INDRA NOOYI
CEO of PepsiCo

Her approach is a reminder that great leaders don't do everything themselves—they build people who can do everything well.

Closing Thoughts

Delegation isn't about doing less; it's about achieving more, together.

When you delegate wisely, you don't lose control—you gain clarity, growth and time for what truly matters.

CHAPTER 5

SELF-CARE: YOUR FOUNDATION FOR SUCCESS

Self-care is often misunderstood, especially by men.

In many families, including my own, I'v9e seen how men are raised to believe that their primary role is to earn, provide and lead. From a young age, they are conditioned to push themselves relentlessly for the sake of their families and businesses. And somewhere along the way, they forget themselves.

I've witnessed this closely in my married family. My father-in-law, N.K. Aggarwal, and my husband, Ajay Aggarwal, are two of the most dedicated and hardworking people I know. Even after achieving financial success, they continued working day and night—not because they had to, but because they felt responsible. And in that process, they often neglected rest, reflection and routine well-being.

Many believe that taking a holiday once or twice a year counts as self-care. But the truth is self-care is not something you schedule occasionally. It's something you practise daily.

It's in how you eat, how you rest, how you breathe between meetings and how you allow yourself space to slow down. Not once in a while, but every day.

What Self-Care Really Means
- Getting enough sleep
- Eating without stress
- Taking small breaks
- Moving your body
- Spending time on things you enjoy, even if it's just for a few minutes

Self-care isn't selfish. It's what keeps you sharp, calm and grounded. When you care for yourself, you lead better, think better, and live better.

 **Reflection Questions**

- Do I do anything daily for myself, beyond my work or responsibilities?
- Am I always postponing rest or reflection for 'later'?
- What small habit can I add this week that nourishes me?

Closing Thoughts

Self-care is not an event. It's a way of living. Take care of yourself—not because you're tired, but so you don't burn out.

CHAPTER 6

FAMILY AND RELATIONSHIPS: THE HEART OF BALANCE

A Moment that Hit Home

One of the most emotional turning points in our family life was when our elder son, Krish, was preparing to leave for boarding school in Dehradun. He was just finishing Grade 6, and from Grade 7 onward, he would be away from home right through to Grade 12. Later, he went abroad for his graduation and post-graduation. It all happened so fast.

I still remember the day we were packing his bags. His uniforms, his books, his pillow—everything neatly folded and stacked. There was excitement for his future, of course, but also a quiet heaviness in the air. That's when Ajay ji, my husband, stood silently by the door, watching his son get ready for this new chapter.

In that moment, it hit him hard. When did he grow up?

He hadn't even realised how quickly the years had gone by.

All those years spent building businesses, chasing growth, being the provider—he hadn't seen Krish grow from a little boy into a young man. The milestones had passed quietly while he was busy in boardrooms and on phone calls. That day, more than anything else, made him pause and reflect deeply on how much he had missed, and how much he didn't want to miss anymore.

What We Learnt

We often tell ourselves there will be time later. After this project. After this quarter. After this year. But children grow fast. Time doesn't wait.

Since then, we've had many conversations with other parents, especially fathers, about this, and I say this with sincerity and love: don't wait.

Spend time with your children while they're still around you. While they still want to share their world with you. Because by the time we realise what we missed, it's often too late.

We work from morning to evening to give our families a better life, to provide them with security, comfort and happiness. Every decision we make, every long day we push through, every risk we take—it's all for them. But somewhere along the way, we often forget the very people we're doing all this for.

We spend our entire day at work, and even when we come home, our mind is still at work. The result? We provide our families with luxuries, but unintentionally rob them of our time. We give our children everything except our presence. This is a reality I've witnessed not just in society at large, but in my own home.

When Work Steals the Moments that Matter

In our society, especially among men, there's a pattern—they miss watching their children grow. They work so hard for their families that they don't get the time to actually be with their families.

My husband, Ajay is one of the most hardworking people I know. He built multiple businesses from scratch, took bold decisions and achieved incredible success. But in doing so, he unknowingly missed the small milestones in our children's lives.

He wasn't there to see them take their first steps, say their first words or learn their first lessons. As a mother, I consider myself lucky, because I was present for those beautiful, ordinary, unforgettable moments. But for Ajay ji, time passed too quickly. One day, he looked at our children—taller, more mature, so grown up—and asked, almost in disbelief,

'When did they grow up?'

That was his wake-up call. In that pause, he realised: Who am I working so hard for, if I haven't even spent time with them? That moment changed something in him. It made him reflect. It made him slow down. And it made both of us re-evaluate how we were balancing our roles as parents and professionals.

True Presence Is the Real Gift

We all want to provide the best for our families. But what they often need the most isn't a bigger house or better gadgets. What they truly crave is time, attention and shared joy.

- A child may not remember the toys you bought, but they'll remember the time you sat on the floor and played with them.
- A spouse may not remember every vacation, but they'll remember the nights you sat and really listened.
- Our parents don't want grand gestures—they want time, respect and presence.

Simple Ways to Reconnect

- Keep your phone away during family time.
- Create daily rituals like family dinners, bedtime stories or morning chai.
- Listen without distraction, even if it's just for 10 minutes.
- Be involved—not just financially, but emotionally.

Reflection Questions

⭐ Are you present with your family, or just providing for them?

⭐ What small change can you make today to reclaim more family time?

⭐ Is there a moment you've missed that you don't want to miss again?

Real-Life Inspiration
Azim Premji: Grounded in Relationships

Despite his business success, **Azim Premji** always stayed deeply rooted in his relationships. He maintained a close bond with his family, particularly his mother, and continued to lead with humility, connection and care. His life reminds us that success doesn't have to come at the cost of personal relationships—the two can coexist beautifully.

AZIM PREMJI
Chairman of
Wipro Ltd

Closing Thoughts

Don't just work for your family. Live with them. Laugh with them. Grow with them. Because in the end, no achievement can replace the time lost with the people who matter most.

CHAPTER 7

GIVING BACK: CREATING A PURPOSE BEYOND PROFIT

There comes a point in every business journey when you begin to ask yourself: why am I doing all this?

In the early stages, we work for survival. Then, we chase growth. But true fulfilment comes when we realise that success is not just about how much we achieve, it's about how much good we can do with it.

At Action, we've always believed that business is not just about making money. It's about making meaning. Growth and giving must go hand in hand.

Progress Tied to Purpose

One of the ways we practise this belief is by tying our company's financial progress to our commitment to education. Every year, as our turnover grows, we increase the number of children we adopt for education outside our workplace. It's our way of ensuring that our growth uplifts others too, especially children who may not otherwise have access to opportunity.

Within our company, we also run scholarship programmes for the children of our in-house staff, especially those who excel in Grade 10, Grade 12 and those pursuing medical careers.

But we don't want to stop here.

Our vision is to support every child connected to our workplace—in any field, based on their dreams, not just our criteria, because we believe every child deserves a chance.

**Create a Culture of Giving—
Together**

We don't believe giving should happen only at the leadership level. We actively encourage our staff to participate in acts of charity, where they can use company funds … company funds allocated for social impact. But more than that, we ask them to involve their entire families, especially their children.

'Take your children with you,' we say. 'Let them see what it feels like to help someone in need. Let that seed of giving be planted early.'

Because when children grow up seeing their parents not just earning, but also giving, they carry that value into their own lives, and that's how we create a future generation that doesn't just seek success, but also shares it.

The Power of Our Channel Partners

Our channel partners are also a big part of our extended family. And we inspire them the same way:

- 'Here's a budget. Use it for charity.'
- 'Don't just donate—go and do something yourself.'
- 'Take your children. Make it a family experience.'

Because we're not here just to earn money together.

We are here to earn blessings together.

The Energy Behind the Money We Earn

At Action, we believe that our life flourishes not just because of how much money we earn, but because of the energy with which that money is earned.

- Was it earned ethically?
- Did it come with goodwill and service?
- Did it help someone rise?

If the answers are yes, then we don't just earn income, we earn grace, peace and fulfilment.

Tool: The Purpose-driven Business Model

Here's how to build giving into your business DNA:

1. Choose a cause: What resonates with your team—education, health, women's and so on?
2. Tie it to success: Link revenue growth with measurable 'goals of giving' would make it clearer.

3. Empower the team: Let employees and partners participate hands-on.
4. Involve the next generation: Encourage families and children to experience giving.
5. Celebrate stories: Share the impact internally because it creates pride and unity.

Real-Life Inspiration
Ratan Tata: Legacy Rooted in Compassion

Ratan Tata, one of India's most admired industrialists, is the perfect embodiment of purpose-led leadership. Under his guidance, the Tata Group not only grew into a global business empire, but also became a symbol of ethical business and deep social responsibility.

RATAN TATA
Chairperson of the Tata Group

Through the Tata Trusts, he has directed a significant portion of the group's profits toward healthcare, education, rural development and social innovation. Even after retirement, his work continues to reflect humility, vision and compassion.

His life reminds us that true success lies not only in building companies, but in building lives, communities and a more compassionate world.

 **Reflection Questions**

- Is your business giving back in a way that feels meaningful?
- How can you involve your team and their families in charitable efforts?
- What kind of values are you passing on to the next generation through your work?

Closing Thoughts

Let the money you earn carry good energy. Let it carry blessings, goodwill and purpose.

Because in the end, the true wealth is not just in profits, it's in people, peace and the lives you uplift along the way.

CHAPTER 8

CONTINUOUS LEARNING: GROWING BEYOND THE ORDINARY

After my wake-up call, when I joined the course my husband recommended, I thought it would be a one-time learning experience. But what I didn't realise then was that I was stepping into something much bigger, a lifelong journey of growth, curiosity and continuous learning.

That first course, conducted by Rahul Jain in 2017, was the turning point. It gave me structure, tools and a shift in perspective. But more than that, it opened the doors to a whole new mindset.

I was one of the youngest participants in the room. Many of my classmates were in their fifties and sixties, already successful in their fields. Yet, there they were, notebooks open, eagerly learning. That's when it struck me:

There is no age to learn. No stage where you 'know it all'. Learning is a way of living.

Learning in a Fast-Changing World

We live in a time where change is the only constant. Technology, people, preferences—everything is evolving. And if we don't keep learning, we don't just fall behind, we remain stuck in the past.

Continuous learning has kept me relevant, agile and forward-looking. That one course led me to many others, and to books and tools that truly shaped who I am today.

> **Some of the most impactful books on my journey:**
> - *The Monk Who Sold His Ferrari* by Robin Sharma: A gentle but powerful call to seek balance and inner peace
> - *The 7 Habits of Highly Effective People* by Stephen Covey: A timeless guide to personal and professional effectiveness

- *Don't Sweat the Small Stuff* by Richard Carlson: This reminded me to breathe and let go of what doesn't truly matter
- *Eat That Frog* by Brian Tracy: A sharp tool for overcoming procrastination and managing time smartly
- *Unlimited Power* by Tony Robbins: This opened my mind to the immense strength of our thoughts, habits and mindset

Beyond books, I began enrolling in workshops and programmes that deepened my growth. I took up Akshar Yadav's 'Get Over Booked', the transformative 'Quantum Leap' programme, and many more that helped me connect the dots between inner clarity and external success.

Each step led to the next. Each insight made life, and leadership, a little lighter, a little wiser.

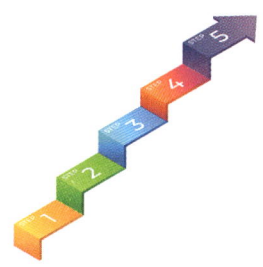

Why Learning Supports Work-Life Balance

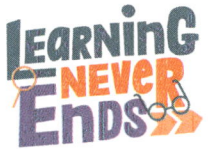

Learning Makes Life Easier:
- It helps you discover smarter ways to work.
- It cuts mental noise and brings sharper decisions.
- It keeps your energy fresh and your ideas flowing.
- It connects you with people who challenge and uplift you.

When we grow, we gain perspective. And when we gain perspective, balance becomes easier to achieve, not just in theory, but in real life.

Tool: The Learning Action Plan

Here's a simple way to build learning into your life:

1. Set aside one hour a week. It's a small investment for a big return.
2. Pick one learning area. It could be leadership, wellness, parenting, finance: whatever speaks to you and can further your growth.

3. Choose your medium: books, courses, podcasts, mentor sessions, webinars.
4. Reflect and apply. Ask yourself, what did I learn, and how can I use it this week?

 **Tip:** Learning is not about how much you consume, it's about how deeply you apply what resonates.

- What's one area of your life that would benefit from new learning?
- Are you making time to grow, or just repeating old routines?
- Who in your circle inspires you to keep learning?

Real-Life Inspiration
Bill Gates: The Power of a Lifelong Learner

Despite all his accomplishments, **Bill Gates** continues to learn like a student. He reads over fifty books a year, dedicates 'think weeks' to reflection and stays curious about everything from healthcare to innovation. He once said, 'Reading is still the main way that I both learn new things and test my understanding.'

BILL GATES
Founder, Microsoft

Gates proves that learning isn't a phase, it's a mindset. And no matter how successful you become, there's always something new to explore.

Closing Thoughts

In a world that never stops changing, the most valuable skill is the ability to keep learning.

No matter your age, title or experience, there is always a next level waiting to be explored.

CHAPTER 9

CREATING A POSITIVE WORKPLACE CULTURE

Successful workplace isn't just built on systems, strategies and sales, it's built on people, energy and purpose. When people feel respected, valued and spiritually grounded, they give their best, not just because they have to, but because they want to. Over the years, I've seen that a workplace filled with good energy, mutual care and shared values becomes not just productive, but powerful.

At Action, we've made it a priority to build a culture that uplifts, centres and strengthens the people who are at the heart of our business—our team.

The Soul of the Workplace

In our offices and factories, we begin the day with prayers and bhajans. It's a moment of peace amidst chaos, of grounding amidst pressure.

It reminds everyone, from workers to management, that we are here not just to produce, but to create with presence and gratitude.

This practice is more than ritual, it's a reflection of our belief that when positive energy flows through a workplace, success follows naturally.

Smiles Over Stress

Another simple but powerful practice we follow at Action is encouraging everyone to wear a smiley badge at work. It may seem small, but that little badge is a reminder to each person that life is about happiness— being happy with yourself and with others.

Since most of our time is spent at work, the workplace shouldn't be a source of stress. It should be a space of joy, connection and personal peace.

When you carry a smile, you carry positive energy, and that energy spreads. It's not just a badge, it's a mindset.

Workplace culture isn't shaped only by strategy, it's shaped by shared memories and joyful connection.

At Action, we don't just work together, we celebrate together.
- We organise monthly birthday celebrations filled with music, dance and fun games.
- We go on team picnics that help us connect beyond roles and responsibilities.
- And one of our most loved traditions is the annual cricket tournament, complete with month-long practice sessions that create a healthy spirit of competition, bonding and energy.

These aren't just events, they are moments of belonging that remind that they're a part of something bigger than their job description.

Empowering Through Inclusion

A positive culture also means inviting everyone to grow. We encourage ideas from all levels of the organisation. Whether it's a new production suggestion from a floor worker or a marketing idea from a young executive, we listen. Because we believe every voice has value. Inclusivity, in our culture, is not a trend, it's a tradition.

Tool: Building a High-Energy Culture

Here's a framework you can use to strengthen workplace culture:

1. Anchor in values. Clearly define what your business stands for: respect, compassion, growth.
2. Create moments of connection, like prayer time, picnics, birthday celebrations or sports events.
3. Recognise effort naturally. A simple 'well done' or public appreciation can go a long way.
4. Listen deeply. Ensure people feel safe, seen and supported.
5. Remind them of the 'why'. Help your team feel connected to a larger purpose, not just daily tasks.

Reflection Questions

- Does your team feel seen, heard and respected at work?
- What small change could make your work environment more joyful and human?
- Are you making space for fun, connection and shared pride?

Real-Life Inspiration
Narayana Murthy: Leading with Simplicity and Integrity

NARAYANA MURTHY
Co-Founder, Infosys

Narayana Murthy, co-founder of Infosys, is one of India's most respected business leaders. What made Infosys stand out wasn't just technology or strategy, it was culture. Murthy believed in building an organisation based on ethics, fairness and humility. He led with transparency, valued every employee's contribution and insisted that success must be rooted in honesty and service.

He lived simply, treated everyone with dignity and built a company where employees felt safe, heard and inspired. His leadership shows us that culture isn't built through slogans or policies, it's built through consistent values, example and intention.

Closing Thoughts

Culture is not what you say, it's what you consistently do.

Build a workplace where people don't just clock in for a job, but arrive with purpose, peace and pride.

CHAPTER 10

THE POWER OF SAYING 'NO'

When we talk about achieving work-life balance, one of the most underrated tools is the ability to say NO. We often assume that balance comes from better scheduling, multitasking or being more organised. But in truth, balance often begins with the courage to decline what doesn't serve your priorities.

Every time you say yes to something unimportant, you might be saying no to something deeply important—your family, your peace, your personal time or your purpose.

Saying no doesn't make you difficult, it makes you disciplined.

Why We Struggle to Say 'No'

In our social and professional lives, saying yes is often seen as respectful and supportive. We say yes to look

And we hesitate to say no because:

- We don't want to disappoint others
- We fear looking rude or unhelpful
- We think saying no may harm our reputation.

good, maintain relationships and sometimes, simply simply to avoid being misunderstood.

But always saying yes can lead to a life full of commitments that don't reflect our true purpose. Balance requires boundaries.

The Ninety Per Cent Rule

One of the most practical tools I've learnt is the 90 Per Cent Rule. When faced with a new request or opportunity, ask, does this align with my values, goals and current focus at a 90 per cent level or more?

If not, say no gracefully.

This rule helps remove emotional pressure and keeps your time and energy focused where they matter most.

How to Say No Gracefully

Saying no doesn't need to be harsh, it can be thoughtful and kind. Here are some ways to do it:

> **'Thank you so much, but I won't be able to take this on right now.'**
> - 'I really appreciate you thinking of me, but I need to decline due to other priorities.'
> - 'This sounds interesting, but I'm unable to commit at the moment.'

Every time you say no to something unimportant, you make room for something meaningful.

What Does Saying No Create Space For?

You don't have to justify your decision with long explanations. A sincere NO is more than enough.

- More time for yourself
- Deeper presence with family
- Better focus on important projects
- Peace of mind and emotional space

Saying NO isn't closing a door, it's just about opening the right one.

 **Reflection Questions**

- Are there things you say yes to out of habit or pressure?

- What's one area where saying 'no' could give you more clarity or freedom?

- How would your life feel with fewer obligations and more intention?

Real-Life Inspiration
Dr. A.P.J. Abdul Kalam—Saying No to Ego, Yes to Purpose

DR. A.P.J. ABDUL KALAM
India's Former President

Dr. A.P.J. Abdul Kalam, India's former President and one of the most respected leaders of our time, lived a life guided by values and simplicity. While he held the highest office in the country and achieved global recognition as a scientist and thinker, he consistently chose purpose over popularity.

He said NO to:
- Lavish lifestyle privileges, even as the president
- Political power plays or preferential treatment
- Commercial endorsements or personal gain
- Events that didn't align with his mission of serving the youth and the nation

Instead, he filled his days with what mattered most to him: teaching, reading, writing and inspiring the younger generation.

'You have to dream before your dreams can come true. But to live your dream, you must have the discipline to say no to what distracts you from it,' Dr Abdul Kalam wrote.

His legacy teaches us that saying no is not rejection, it's protection of your deepest purpose.

Closing Thoughts

NO is not a negative word. It's a powerful boundary that protects your energy, your priorities and your peace.

CHAPTER 11

SYSTEMS, TECHNOLOGY AND THE POWER OF DOING IT RIGHT

In the fast-moving world we live in, not every company is fully tech-driven, but even small shifts towards systems and structure can bring surprising ease to work and life. I've experienced this first-hand.

For many years, our company operated in the same way, relying on pen and paper for everything. Orders, dispatches, stock, store management—everything was done manually. It was the way we had always worked. But over time, we realised that we were already late in adopting technology.

So we decided to take a step forward. We enrolled in a few courses, upskilled ourselves and started introducing some basic systems. We also trained our team, teaching them how to use simple tools and reports. Slowly, we incorporated MIS systems, computerised reporting and began tracking everything digitally. From sales and production to purchases and inventory—every stage became clearer and more structured. And the results were eye-opening.

The same staff, once equipped with new knowledge, started bringing far more value to the company. The reports helped us take quicker, more informed decisions. Day-to-day work became smoother. Accountability improved. And as a team, we began functioning with more clarity and confidence. We still have a long way to go. But even that little start brought a big shift. It proved that technology doesn't need to be complicated, it just needs to be aligned with the intent to improve.

We've always believed in clean and transparent business practices—working the right way, with proper systems, documentation and compliance. Our company has always operated in white money. Because of this, even large-scale changes like demonetisation and GST didn't create chaos for us. We were already aligned with structure, so we didn't have to scramble. We were prepared, and that gave us something very precious—peace of mind.

In business, many chase short-term profits by cutting corners or working informally. But in doing so, they often trade away their clarity, peace and long-term potential. Over time, the cost of that trade becomes very visible, not just in the stress it creates, but in how difficult it becomes to scale, delegate or eventually hand over the business to the next generation.

When there are no systems, there is no clarity. And when there is no clarity, there is no inheritance, only confusion.

I truly believe that building simple systems and embracing even basic technology—whether it's reporting tools, SOPs, or digital tracking—can help you build not just a company, but a legacy.

Closing Thoughts

Sometimes we trade our peace of mind for a little extra money. But over time, that trade costs us more than we gain.

CHAPTER 12

WEALTH MANAGEMENT: SECURING YOUR FUTURE

Success is not just about building a business or earning more, it's about managing wealth with wisdom. Because earning money is only the first step. What you do with it determines the kind of life you live and the legacy you leave. In my journey, I've seen both people who earned well but lost it due to poor management, and those who built sustainable wealth through clarity, discipline and planning.

Wealth is not just for comfort. It is for freedom, security, contribution and continuity. Wealth that works for you, and beyond you!

True wealth should:
- Give you peace of mind
- Protect your family during tough times
- Allow you to explore opportunities
- Support causes that matter to you
- Continue to serve future generations

The Three Pillars of Wise Wealth Management

1. *Wealth Creation—Growing Your Assets*

> **Wealth begins with earning, but it grows with strategy.**
> - *Diversify your income:* Don't rely on one business or one source. Explore real estate, investments and new ideas.
> - *Invest in growth assets:* Mutual funds, equity and long-term real estate are key for future security.
> - *Use strategic borrowing:* Use loans for expansion or appreciating assets, not for luxury or lifestyle.

Example: Mukesh Ambani scaled Reliance by diversifying into telecom and digital, and not staying limited to oil.

2. Wealth Protection—Safeguarding What You've Built

> **Even strong businesses face risks. Protection is about stability.**
> - *Emergency fund:* Always keep 6–12 months of expenses saved.
> - *Insurance:* Health, life and business insurance are non-negotiable.
> - *Legal and financial structure:* Create trusts, wills and financial plans for long-term safety.

For example, the Tata Group maintains reserves and has structured its trusts to ensure business and social continuity.

3. Wealth Growth—Making Money Work While You Rest

> **Let your money multiply quietly and consistently.**
> - *Follow the 50-30-20 rule:* 50% Needs | 30% Lifestyle | 20% Investment

- *Understand compounding:* Start investing early. The longer money stays invested, the more it grows.
- *Balance your portfolio:* Don't put everything in one place—spread your money across equity, real estate, fixed income and future ventures.

Example: Rakesh Jhunjhunwala built a fortune through simple, long-term investing and patience.

Learning from Mistakes: What Not To Do

Overspending and Lifestyle Inflation

Success often brings temptation. But wealth disappears fast when it's spent faster than it's earned.

Emotional Financial Decisions

Don't chase every trend or react in fear. Be calm, informed and disciplined.

No Plan for Future Generations

If wealth is not protected by a structure, it can lead to conflict, confusion or loss.

Example: Kingfisher Airlines collapsed due to financial mismanagement and over-leveraging.

Legacy Planning: Beyond Numbers

Wealth isn't just about your lifestyle, it's about your impact.
- *Teach financial literacy to the next generation:* Equip your children to value and manage wealth.
- *Give back:* Allocate a portion of profits for social causes because it brings meaning to money.
- *Succession planning:* Decide who manages what. Discuss it and document it clearly to avoid future tension.

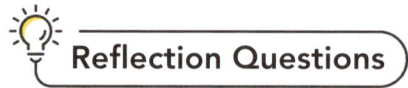

Reflection Questions

- 💡 Are you diversifying your income and investments wisely?
- 💡 Do you have clear protection and backup plans?
- 💡 Are you planning wealth not just for yourself, but for the next generation and for society?

Real-Life Inspiration
Savitri Jindal—Wealth with Values and Legacy

Savitri Jindal, the matriarch of the Jindal Group and India's richest woman, represents the true spirit of generational wealth managed with strong values. After the passing of her husband, she took on the leadership of the business with grace. And today, the Jindal family continues to run multiple successful businesses with a focus on unity, tradition and philanthropy.

SAVITRI JINDAL
India's Richest Woman

She's known not only for her business acumen but for her commitment to social causes, education and community development. Under her guidance, the Jindal legacy has expanded across industries while staying grounded in family values.

Her story reminds us that wealth is not just a financial asset, it is a responsibility, a value system and a gift to be protected and passed on with care.

Closing Thoughts

It's not how much you earn. It's how you manage, multiply and share what you earn that defines your wealth.

CHAPTER 13

LIVING THE BALANCE

A Gentle Closing to a Lifelong Practice

Balance is not a destination, it's a way of living.

It's not something we achieve once and then forget. It's something we build, lose, rebuild and refine over and over again. Some weeks, we feel aligned and focused. Other weeks, life demands more from one area, and something else slips. That's okay. That's real life.

This book was never meant to be a strict blueprint. It is a collection of reflections, stories, tools and learnings from my own journey, offered with honesty and hope. I wrote it during a period of deep reflection, far from home, in a different time zone, watching my team flourish in my absence. It reminded me that systems, trust, support and surrender create the space for balance to breathe.

But even more than systems, balance is about consciousness.

What living the balance looks like:
- It's saying no when something doesn't align with you.
- It's trusting your team, and letting go of the urge to control everything.
- It's spending Sunday evening with your children, not your inbox.
- It's showing up for your parents.
- It's nourishing your mind and body, not just your business.
- It's allowing others to grow alongside you.
- It's remembering, always, that success without presence is incomplete.

Let this be a reminder:

You don't need to do everything. You don't need to be everywhere. You don't need to prove anything.
You are allowed to slow down without losing your spark.

You are allowed to grow at your own pace. You are allowed to define success on your own terms.

A Few Simple Practices to Keep You Centred:

1. *Weekly check-ins:*
   Ask: What do I need more of? What do I need less of?
2. *Celebrate small wins:*
   Balance is often hidden in the little choices we make each day.
3. *Keep learning:*
   One podcast, one page or one idea a week is enough.
4. *Pause often:*
   Even a few minutes of silence between meetings can reset your energy.
5. *Return to your 'why':*
   When you feel off-balance, come back to your purpose.